Jonah

Illustrated Lyrics of Faith

Based on the song by Joe Guadagno

Hear the song on Spotify!	Hear the song on Apple Music!	Hear the song on YouTube!

by Joe Guadagno
and Victoria Winifred

Jonah:
Illustrated Lyrics of Faith
©2024 Joe Guadagno and Victoria Winifred.

Published by The Enrichment Connection.
Paperback ISBN: 979-8-9915289-0-0
1st Edition

All Rights Reserved. No part of this book may be reproduced or transmitted in any form or by any means whatsoever without express written permission from the author, except in the case of brief quotations embodied in critical articles and reviews. Please refer all pertinent questions to The Enrichment Connection at enrichmentconnection@gmail.com.

DISCLAIMER: This work is based on biblical content and includes lyrics from the song "Jonah," written, recorded, and copyrighted by the author, Joe Guadagno. While the characters, places, events, and incidents may be inspired by the scripture, they have been adapted and reinterpreted by the author. Any resemblance to actual persons, living or dead, outside of the biblical context, is purely coincidental. This work also includes passages from the Bible. All Scripture quotations are from the King James Version (KJV), which is in the public domain.

All cover and interior artwork was output by Canva's Magic Media and edited in Photoshop.

All of Joe Guadagno's music is available on most major music streaming platforms, either under his name or his band's name, JGnFriends.

Remember that
even from the depths,
God will hear your prayers
and guide you back
to your
rightful path.

He found a ship in Joppa, paid his fare and went on board, and Jonah sailed to Tarshish as he tried to flee the Lord.

But a great big wind blew a violent storm
sent by God's own hand,
and every man aboard then wondered
if they'd ever see dry land.

They tried to reach the coastline, they tried to no avail,

and these hardened sailors cried aloud and they began to wail.

Well, the Lord he answered Jonah, and the great fish spit him out.

He went where God commanded, gave God's message with a shout!

and there was joy in Ninevah, God's mercy they received!

If you're like Jonah, you better go and change your mind!
If you're resisting what the Lord's insisting,
well, you're going to have a whale of a time.
You're going to have a whale of a time!

The Biblical Verses Behind the Lyrics

Jonah 1:2 (KJV):
"Arise, go to Nineveh...."

Jonah 1:3 (KJV):
"But Jonah rose up to flee unto Tarshish from the presence of the LORD, and went down to Joppa; and he found a ship going to Tarshish: so he paid the fare..."

Jonah 1:12 (KJV):
"And he said unto them...cast me forth into the sea...for I know that for my sake this great tempest is upon you."

Jonah 1:15 (KJV):
"So they took up Jonah, and cast him forth into the sea: and the sea ceased from her raging."

Jonah 1:17 (KJV):
"Now the LORD had prepared a great fish to swallow up Jonah. And Jonah was in the belly of the fish three days and three nights."

Jonah 2:1-2 (KJV):
"Then Jonah prayed unto the LORD his God out of the fish's belly..."

Jonah 2:10 (KJV):
"And the LORD spake unto the fish, and it vomited out Jonah upon the dry land."

Jonah 3:4
"And Jonah began to enter into the city ...and said, Yet forty days, and Nineveh shall be overthrown."

Jonah 3:5
"So the people of Nineveh believed God..."

Jonah 3:10 (KJV):
"And God saw ...that they turned from their evil way; and God repented of the evil, that he had said that he would do unto them; and he did it not."

Questions for Discussion:

Understanding the Story:
Why did Jonah try to go to Tarshish instead of going to Nineveh as God told him?

Exploring Actions:
What did Jonah do when he was inside the fish, and how did he change during that time?

Personal Reflection:
Have you ever avoided doing something you knew you should do? How did it make you feel? What happened as a result?

Thinking Deeper:
How do Jonah's actions and attitudes before and after he was in the fish show us about changing our minds and accepting responsibility?

Applying the Lesson:
How can the story of Jonah help you handle a situation where you're reluctant to do something you know is important or right?

Reflect on Jonah's experience and his journey after running away from God's calling. Take a moment to write your own prayer. Use this opportunity to express gratitude, seek forgiveness, or ask for guidance, inspired by the lessons of repentance and divine compassion in Jonah's story.

_____

_____

_____

_____

_____

_____

_____

_____

_____

_____

The Illustrated Lyrics of Faith Series

The Illustrated Lyrics of Faith series features picture books for the family based on the scripturally-based Christian songs of singer/songwriter Joe Guadagno.

Other titles in this series include:

The Prodigal Son

What Are You Waiting For?

One Touch

Climb That Mountain

Father Knows Best

Eyes of a Miracle

www.ingramcontent.com/pod-product-compliance
Lightning Source LLC
Chambersburg PA
CBHW060807090426
42736CB00002B/187